T0146566

Power Over Pain

The POP Method for Whole-Body Healing

Dr. Michelle DiBiase

BALBOA.
PRESS

A DIVISION OF HAY HOUSE

Balboa Press books may be ordered through booksellers or by contacting:

Balboa Press
A Division of Hay House
1663 Liberty Drive
Bloomington, IN 47403
www.balboapress.com
1 (877) 407-4847

Because of the dynamic nature of the Internet, any web addresses or links contained in this book may have changed since publication and may no longer be valid. The views expressed in this work are solely those of the author and do not necessarily reflect the views of the publisher, and the publisher hereby disclaims any responsibility for them.

The information, ideas, and suggestions in this book are not intended as a substitute for professional medical advice or treatment. The intent of this author is only to offer information of a general nature to help you on your journey of physical, emotional and spiritual balance and well-being. Neither the author nor the publisher shall be liable or responsible for any consequence resulting from the action of using information or suggestions in this book.

Any people depicted in stock imagery provided by Thinkstock are models, and such images are being used for illustrative purposes only. Certain stock imagery © Thinkstock.

Print information available on the last page.

ISBN: 978-1-5043-4437-1 (sc)
ISBN: 978-1-5043-4439-5 (hc)
ISBN: 978-1-5043-4438-8 (e)

Library of Congress Control Number: 2015918765

Balboa Press rev. date: 11/19/2015

To my love and my light,
John, Ruby and Isabelle
You are my greatest blessings and
most precious gifts.

To my readers,
May you reach your highest potential and manifest
your most extraordinary dreams. Your inner self is
always perfect, even if your outer self doesn't reflect
it. May this method let your inner light shine.

Contents

The soul has been given its own ears to hear things that the mind does not understand.

—Rumi

Preface

Have you ever wondered why some people have terrible pain and others do not, even when the circumstances are the same? For instance, two people are in a car accident; one person walks away feeling fine, and the other has chronic pain for years. Why is that?

As a chiropractor, I see people every day who have chronic, debilitating pain. With some, their spines look horrible and there is a clear correlation between the structure and the function. But with others, the structure isn't that bad, but the pain is devastating! Do those people just have a low pain tolerance? Or is there something else to blame?

This book is designed to tackle that question— to give a way of handling these problems so they don't continue to come back. Is pain really about dysfunction? Or is there another reason that some feel things differently than others? Maybe the feelings and the emotions around the pain are the real problem, and maybe if those feelings change, so will the pain.

Time and time again I have had people come to me with pain they have had for years. Many times I was the last resort. With some I could see a clear correlation between their symptoms and their clinical findings, but many times, the connection just wasn't there. And why would some people respond so quickly to treatment but others, with the same symptoms and findings, would take months to get relief? It just didn't add up. There had to be another factor.

Then I found the missing link. From studying various methodologies and techniques that addressed the emotional side of dysfunction and disease, I realized that dealing with the feelings around the pain was what was missing from current treatment. The elephant in the room was not even being addressed! Until the emotions and feelings *behind* the pain were brought to light and dealt with, the pain could improve, but it would eventually return.

Even though the majority of my patients got great results with traditional treatment methods, there were still some who didn't respond as I expected them to. I couldn't sit by and watch the ones who didn't respond as quickly continue to suffer from chronic pain and problems. I didn't want to be another doctor who told them that it was all in their heads and not give them a way to fix it. I had to address the missing link.

For me, the most rewarding part of my job as a chiropractor is giving people the ability to live their lives to their highest potential. That's why I became a doctor in the first place. What I was searching for was a method that would have easy, reproducible steps to deal with the emotional issues once and for all. I wanted a way for the patient to heal physically, mentally, and spiritually but also a method that could be done in the comfort of their own homes at their own pace. I not only wanted people to live pain-free but also to live their lives as the most perfect version of themselves that they could be.

I spent many nights meditating and praying about this idea. I had learned several techniques to help pinpoint key emotions and treat them and had remarkable success with it with patients in the office, but in order to resolve some of the tougher cases, I needed a more thorough process to get lasting results. And when I tried to teach some of the concepts to patients so they could work on these issues on their own at home, they never seemed to be able to get the same results. I needed a step-by-step system.

So one day, during my daily meditation, I asked for this step-by-step process to help my patients. And the method became clear. It just literally popped into my head. (It really is the POP Method!) Once I had the steps and started going through this process with people, they could finally get it and do it themselves, right from home. I finally had my answer—a reproducible method for people to finally have *Power Over Pain*—and with it, a way to approach pain relief physically, mentally, and spiritually.

This book is for those of you who are at the end of your rope. This book is for those of you who have tried everything and nothing has worked. But this book is also for those who want a new way to handle life's problems. It's a way to overcome the challenges the world sends your way by discovering the thoughts and feelings that are hurting you and letting them go for good. Now there is a step-by-step approach to handle pain from the inside out—a method of getting to the emotional root that may be anchoring you to the pain. This process also gives a way to see these feelings in a new light and to allow them to be let go.

The POP Method focuses on the "feeling" component of pain, an often-overlooked but significant part of our health. The process also allows us to connect and explore the part of us that is perfect, what I like to call our spirit/soul self, and remove the emotions that may have tarnished that version of ourselves and in turn, caused chronic pain to settle in.

This is not a religious book per se, but being balanced physically, emotionally, and spiritually is, in my opinion, crucial for overall health and well-being. I have found that when a person will explore and work through all three of these things, that's when the magic happens. In essence, the POP Method helps us find the stored emotions, change the way they are viewed and the way our bodies physically manifest them, and then let it all go by allowing our spiritual selves to take it away. As a result, our bodies will be in perfect balance.

If you are a person of faith, this method gives power to your prayers. If you are not, you can still benefit from this work because it gives you a process of getting to the feelings that can be keeping you from healing while also giving you a way to let them go. You don't have to be religious to find this method useful, but because of my beliefs, I refer to God in this book to assist in releasing and removing the emotional roots and the pain.

When I first developed this method for pain relief, I struggled with how to introduce it to my patients. I wondered if they would be open to the idea that their feelings could be causing their pain to keep coming back. As I said earlier, I have always known that having all aspects of ourselves in balance (physical, emotional, and spiritual) is crucial, but I was still hesitant to delve too deeply into it. Living in South Georgia, the Bible belt, as it is known, having faith is the rule, not the exception. But bringing feelings, emotions, and spiritual connection into the patient conversation was a step I wasn't sure I was ready to take.

Although I was hesitant, I knew that the POP Method would address those missing components of our traditional treatment methods. Our world is in a healthcare crisis, and a different approach to healing is needed now. So although at first it was difficult to start that emotional and spiritual dialogue, once I began using the steps, the patients began to see their bodies in a whole new light.

This method gives you five simple steps. With these five simple steps, the pain can be history. With these five simple steps, your life will change. As the saying goes, when you look at life differently, your life becomes different. It's time to look at pain differently and to release its hold on us for good. It's time to get Power over the Pain.

We cannot solve our problems with the same thinking we used when we created them.

—Albert Einstein

CHAPTER 1

What Is Pain Really?

B efore we begin the process of eliminating your pain, let's first take a look at what pain really is. Just for a moment, imagine a life where pain is nonexistent. You wake up, jump out of bed, and feel great. You are running late though, and because of your rush, you trip on the way into the bathroom, landing face-first on the floor. It doesn't hurt a bit, so it doesn't slow you down and you keep on going. You continue on to get ready for the day, heading into the shower. The water is steamy, scalding to the point of blistering your skin, but you don't really notice it because you feel no pain. You later head to the kitchen to make yourself breakfast, and in your rush to not be late for work, you accidentally cut your hand wide open, and blood is dripping everywhere! But no worries, it doesn't hurt, so you just put a bandage on it and head out to your job. Do you see where I'm going with this? When you think about pain this way, would you consider that pain may not be your enemy but instead, it may be your protector?

Many times pain is an indicator—a warning, if you will. It lets us know on the outside that there is something wrong on the inside. It's a message telling us that our bodies have had enough. It's the result, the effect, of something else.

When we are discussing pain, we need to talk about the different types of pain there are. When an injury or event first occurs, the pain that is experienced is considered acute pain. Many times this type of pain, if treated soon after the injury, will go away with traditional methods. But when left to its own devices and fueled by the emotions associated with it, it becomes what is called chronic pain or suffering pain. Even though the POP Method works with acute injuries as well, especially when we can easily identify the initial emotions we associate with the injury, the type of pain we are really focusing on in this book is the chronic type.

The development of chronic pain is a process, and it isn't the result of just one thing. Of course, if you are in an accident and have pain immediately, you know that the primary cause can be directly traced back to that trauma, the acute pain reaction, but if the pain lingers on and on, well past the treatment plan and the customary time it takes a person to heal from an injury, that's chronic pain.

Maybe you got some relief but never felt like the problem was resolved. That lingering pain was still a result of the accident, but maybe it was not from the physical nature of the wreck but instead from the emotions surrounding the event. Pain can develop from the *feeling* part of your body, and if that part isn't addressed, the pain keeps coming back.

Pain lets your conscious mind know that something is wrong. It's like the warning light on the dashboard of your car. When we see the light come on, do we just cover it up and keep on driving without addressing the reason the light came on in the first place? Of course that sounds ridiculous to us because with our cars, we know we have to correct the problem that *caused* the light to come on or our car will eventually break down. Just like our cars, our bodies provide a warning signal, and although we want the pain alleviated quickly and easily, if we only address that outer symptom, or warning light, if you will, and ignore the underlying feelings that fuel it, the pain will continue to come back. And furthermore, what other problems are going to result because of that initial issue?

Usually when I introduce the POP Method to patients and explain the concept of the process, the knee-jerk response is that they can't think of any emotion or feeling that they connect to the pain. Even past that, they can't fathom why they would hold on to something that caused them grief and would result in chronic pain. The majority of people I encounter who have chronic pain just attribute it to age or some activity that they did for so many years. While overexertion and repetitive physical activities over a course of time can be the culprit, if the pain is not responding to traditional methods, chiropractic or medical, then there has to be something else keeping it active.

Let's consider this: could it be possible that working for so many years doing some activity for all those years made you feel frustrated, angry, disrespected, and so on, and those feelings are keeping that pain tied to you? It's a different way to think about your pain, isn't it? Sometimes it's hard to believe that our feelings about our circumstances, our work, or any event, for that matter, could be keeping us chained to the pain. It's hard to imagine that our feelings on the inside can be reflected physically as feelings on the outside, but many times, that is the reality.

To get a better understanding of how emotions and feelings can anchor pain, I want you to think of the difference between how a child responds to an injury versus an adult. When young children have a fall, for example, they respond to the actual sensation they have as a reaction to the fall. If it doesn't really hurt, they get up and get moving again. No problem. If they do experience some pain, they may cry initially and be upset about it, but then once they begin to get involved in some other activity and their minds wander, the boo-boo is forgotten.

On the other hand, when adults fall down, all different kinds of emotions can come up. Maybe at first they experience the shock of falling, then the possible embarrassment of someone seeing them or the fear that they might have broken something. Maybe they worry that they won't get better quickly or that it is going to keep them from the activities they love to do. They are already creating a mental picture of this incident causing lasting pain and problems. Can you see the difference? Of course, this analogy does not always hold true, but I'm using it to establish that we, as adults, have many emotions that can get tied in with an injury and with our pain.

One of the main reasons why we have such trouble identifying our feelings is because, as a society, we have been made to believe we shouldn't express them. We have become stuffers—we stuff our true feelings down deep and act as if everything is just fine. For a while, that works out all right, but eventually too much has been stuffed in and it begins to erupt. Those feelings must be dealt with, and in our bodies, if it's not, all of that stress and turmoil inside becomes an outward manifestation instead … namely, chronic pain.

Think of the millions upon millions of sufferers who are out in the world each day. Why do so many people hurt? The answer could be that we have never dealt with the feelings we have buried within us! Those feelings have transformed into something physical, and our bodies are begging us to do something. The warning light is glowing, and it is time to look for the cause.

Let's think about this for a moment. Typically, what is our response when the pain begins? In most cases, we go to the doctor, have someone evaluate our symptoms, and then treat them. Does that work? Sometimes it may, maybe at least for the short term, but until the root cause is eliminated, your body will always suffer. If the traditional medical model worked, our healthcare system wouldn't be where it is today. We are a sick world, especially here in the United States.

With my chiropractic background, my philosophy is different from the medical model. The foundation of treatment revolves around the controlling system of our bodies—the nervous system. If the nervous system isn't working properly, then the rest of the body cannot function properly. Because the nervous system is comprised of the brain and spinal cord, and the skull and spine protect those areas, we adjust the spine, and in turn, the nervous system function improves. Chiropractic treatment gets to the root of many problems by correcting the interference to this controlling system, and as a result, the body heals. We don't treat the symptoms per se but instead address the disruption to the nervous system and the function of the body improves.

But taking these principles of healing one step further, I consider the nervous system to be our feeling system. It interprets every stimulus we experience, whether it is something we feel physically or mentally, and then it responds accordingly. With it being our controlling system, if it's not working properly, the other systems are compromised as well.

Part of our nervous system is our autonomic or automatic part of the system. This is the part that controls breathing, heart rate, digestion, and so on—all the things your body does that you don't have to think about to control. Making up the autonomic part of the system is the sympathetic NS, which is also termed the fight-or-flight part, and the parasympathetic NS, which is also known as the feed-or-breed System. When a strong emotion comes in, such as fear, anger, or frustration, the nervous system's fight-or-flight system registers a threat and takes over. As a result, heart rate and respiration increase, blood flow increases in the muscle tissue, digestion slows, and other body responses happen that would help make our bodies ready to fight or flee. That's exactly what we need when there is imminent danger, but what if the strong emotion was because you got upset about the extra load at work or embarrassed about a slip and fall in front of a group of people? Do you really need the body to react in that manner?

What also happens when strong emotions or other stressors trigger that type of sympathetic response is that the system can get so overloaded with the daily stress we incur and the added emotional trigger that it becomes jammed, and the balance with the other part of the autonomic system (the feed-or-breed) side becomes distorted. At this point, you are no longer digesting food properly, and your hormones are getting imbalanced as a result, all because of those feelings and stressors that your body is detecting.

Over time, as our emotions and feelings cause this system to get overloaded and imbalanced, disease in the body results. Let me give you an example. Suzie came into my office with debilitating shoulder pain. She had it for years, and no matter what she did, it wouldn't let up. She came in to see me for chiropractic treatment and would feel better after every visit, but the problem would soon return. When I asked her if she could identify any emotion or feeling she could relate to the pain, all she could come up with was stress. She said there wasn't really a particular event or feeling that she could think of that she had when the pain started, and when she looked at a list of emotions, she said there were several that described her, but she couldn't see a connection between those feelings and her pain. We then looked at a list of common pain patterns that relate to particular emotions and found that shoulder pain could manifest from family and money stress. To that, she said, "Doesn't everyone have that? I don't think I'm any more stressed than anyone else about those things." (Typical stuffer dialogue.) Just for a starting point, I asked her to come up with what emotion she thought was the most predominant in her life at that moment. She decided that frustration was pretty high on that list, so we started with that.

The minute she voiced that she was frustrated and let that feeling be voiced, I could see the tension in her body increase. And the more I allowed her to talk about her feelings about her life in general, the more the pain flared. This type of reaction is common for people who are stuffers because they don't put any weight in their feelings. They have been taught to disregard their feelings, so they have a hard time even talking about them at all. With Suzie being a stuffer, she had refused to acknowledge a lot of the feelings that were inside. And the more feelings that got stuffed, the harder it was for her body to cope.

Once she was able to recognize that there were some feelings behind the pain, we were able to face the real problem head on and get rid of the pain once and for all. And the steps of the POP Method that are in this book will allow you to do the same.

Let's take a minute to determine if you are or have been a stuffer. Here are some key questions to help you:

- Do you consider yourself a rational person rather than an emotional one?
- Do you focus on taking care of others instead of yourself?
- Do you have trouble looking at yourself in the mirror and feeling good about what you see?

- Do you have recurring pain that isn't easily managed?
- Do you have trouble sharing your feelings with others?
- Do you feel uncomfortable in your own skin, so to speak?
- Do you have trouble dealing with other people's emotions?

If you answered *yes* to any of these questions, then I ask you to consider the possibility that you may benefit from some emotional exploration. You may not see a connection to your current pain right away, but as we move through the process, perhaps you will find a connection that you simply haven't noticed. Then, as you begin to recognize that there may be feelings inside festering and bring a voice to them, you are one step closer to becoming the healthy, vibrant, perfect person you were always meant to be.

The moment you change your perception is the moment you rewrite the chemistry of your body.

—Bruce Lipton

CHAPTER 2

The Roots of Chronic Pain

What if the state of our bodies—their function, appearance, and overall health—were primarily determined by our subconscious thoughts? What if what we learned from our parents and from our upbringing shaped our lives and our bodies? In all actuality, a new science called epigenetics has begun to demonstrate how our bodies are not completely controlled by the genes we have been born with but more so by the environment we expose those genes to. And when we are talking about our environment, it is not only the place we live but also the habits we have formed, the ideas we have developed, the feelings that we have, and the way we choose to live our lives that can change the way our genes respond. Our emotional experiences can actually change our DNA. The findings of this branch of science have flipped what we originally believed to be true about how genes affect our bodies and our health, and in many ways, they put the responsibility for our health back in our own hands.

Renowned cellular biologist Dr. Bruce Lipton is a leading authority of epigenetics and how emotions can regulate genetic expression. In his best-selling books *The Biology of Belief* and *Spontaneous Evolution*, he discusses in depth how we are not victims of our heredity. Our health outcomes are not predetermined. In Dr. Lipton's research he has found that our thoughts, diet, and lifestyle can control how our genes respond. We are not destined to die of a heart attack just because our family members before us have. It's how we choose to live our lives and the way we believe, act, and think about our health that determines our outcome.

In Lipton's book *Spontaneous Evolution,* he explains how epigenetics has changed the way we view genes. He describes our genes as blueprints. In essence, he says they are the design drawings, but they are not the contractors that actually construct the building. The genes do not *control* our biology but are instead *used by* biology.

Dr. Lipton discusses how a person can be born healthy, but through a distortion caused by his or her environment (lifestyle choices, stress levels, beliefs, and so on), they can develop something like cancer. But a person born with a gene sequence that could cause potentially debilitating mutations can in turn create healthy and normal genes. Your life experiences can determine what your genetic makeup becomes.

Oftentimes when patients begin care with me, they will say that they knew they would eventually have back pain because their parents suffered for years with the same problem. In their eyes, it was inevitable. But consider this. If you grew up in your parents' home, learned how to walk and talk and live like them, wouldn't you have many of the same patterns? Did you learn from them what to eat, what activities to do, and so on? Does it have to be your genetics, or could you just be having the same symptoms and problems because you have their same habits? It's a different way to look at it, but it makes sense, doesn't it? Also, many of the beliefs and thoughts your parents had became your own beliefs and thoughts. They may not have originally been your beliefs and thoughts, and maybe they weren't originally even your parents' beliefs, but you heard them enough for them to become yours as well. As a result, those beliefs and thoughts created outcomes in your life too. Do you see a pattern here? It may not be genetics that are the true culprit at all.

I know this way of thinking about our health really puts a lot of responsibility on our shoulders. We control our own destiny. And most of us like to put the responsibility elsewhere. It sure seemed better when we could blame it on our parents, right? Well, although passing the blame onto another may have been the way we approached things before, it just isn't our truth anymore. Our health is in our hands. We have to take control of our actions, and that all starts with our beliefs and the truths we tell ourselves each and every day.

Feelings are things, and these things produce and create. Many times we have feelings running in the background of our minds that we aren't even aware of. And those very thoughts and feelings have set us on a path that is very destructive to our bodies.

For years I had to battle my weight. Up and down my weight would go, and I became very frustrated. I tried every diet and exercise program known to man, and nothing seemed to help. I would follow a diet program, lose a few pounds, and start to feel good, and then, before I knew it, I was back to my old habits and my weight was back up.

I finally discovered that these patterns were something running on autopilot behind the scenes of my mind. Thoughts like *I'll never have the body I want, so why should I deprive myself?* or, *It's too hard to stay on a program. I miss out on too much!* I had the belief that weight gain and a slow metabolism were just part of the aging process. These beliefs and feelings and patterns that were running on autopilot in my mind were sabotaging my every move! By identifying these feelings and asking the tough questions, I was able to change those thoughts and feelings. By using this same technique that I'm teaching now, I dealt with the thoughts and emotions behind my weight, those situations that still got an emotional charge out of me, and as a result, I was able to lose the weight and keep it off.

Think about what you tell yourself about your health and your body. What beliefs have you set up within you?

Questions to consider:

- Do you believe that pain is a part of getting older?
- Do you believe that your parents' health problems will probably carry on to you?
- Do you believe that you have little control over your health?
- Do you believe that your pain is probably never going to get better?
- Do you believe that your lifestyle choices are too hard to change?

If you answered *yes* to any of these questions, your beliefs could be sabotaging your health. Take a moment to ask yourself, are those beliefs really even true?

So now that we have discovered through epigenetics that we can change our DNA, and we now know that our lifestyle, our habits, and our beliefs can change the way our bodies feel and function, it's now time to explore how we can make this work in our favor, especially when it comes to our thoughts and feelings.

The Five Steps of the POP Method

Step 1: Identifying the Emotional Anchor

This initial step involves exploring and discovering what was going on at the time the pain started, the feelings that were initially felt, and the feelings and emotions that may have developed as a result of the pain becoming a long-term problem.

Step 2: Asking the Tough Questions

Here we take the emotions we discovered from the previous step and realize why those emotions have formed roots. We ask some difficult questions and examine how we may have held on to these feelings and allowed them to be anchored because, on some level, they serve us in some way or even give us an excuse for being who we are.

Step 3: Reframing the Pain

Once we realize how and why these thoughts and feelings have become anchored, we take those thoughts and beliefs and find a way to reframe and reshape them in our minds. We allow those emotional roots to lose some of their strength in this step.

Step 4: Practicing Gratitude

We continue to loosen and uproot those emotional anchors in this step by finding ways to practice gratitude for all situations and circumstances in our lives—the good and the bad. In this step, we begin to develop a daily practice to flood ourselves with positive feelings and energy, allowing the creation of more expansion of goodness in our lives, and leaving no room for those emotional roots.

Step 5: Releasing

From identifying the root emotions, discovering why they are anchored, reframing those feelings and practicing gratitude for all of our opportunities and gifts, we have now loosened up the hold that those feelings have over us to release them and let them go.

And the pain goes away ...

The power is in you. The answer is in you. And you are the answer to all your searches: You are the goal. You are the answer. It's never outside.

—Eckhart Tolle

CHAPTER 3

Step 1: Identifying the Emotional Anchor

Now it is time to get to work. We have to really dig deep and find the real reason the pain started in the first place and determine why it is holding on. As we spoke about in the previous chapter, many of us are stuffers, and we haven't allowed ourselves to think about how we feel.

In order to find that root emotion, that emotional anchor, if you will, the first step is to really think about your pain. Really hone in on it and focus your attention there. The best way to start is by focusing on the physical aspects of the pain. How does it really feel? Does it feel sharp, dull, achy, tingling, burning, and so on? Focus on that feeling. When you really think about the feeling of the pain, does any emotion come to mind? What is the first thought that pops into your mind? Perhaps you feel angry you even have the pain at all. Or maybe you are scared of what the pain means. Whatever emotions or feelings come to you, note them. These feelings may have nothing to do with the pain itself but may be related in some way to why the problem started in the first place. Even if you see no relation to the pain you are having, it's important to explore it.

To give you some examples of anchoring emotions, I have included a list for you to look at. Sometimes if you look at the list, certain emotions will just jump out at you. Those are the ones you should delve into a little deeper as you move through the process.

Afraid (fear of letting go, fear of failure, fear of the future)	Empty	Sad
Alone	Exhausted	Trapped
Angry	Frustrated	Worried
Annoyed	Grief Stricken	Worthless
Anxious	Heartbroken	Worn Out
Ashamed	Helpless	Uncertain
Bad	Hopeless	Unappreciated

Betrayed	Humiliated	Unloved
Cheated	Hurt	Unmotivated
Concerned	Impatient	Unsure
Confused	Inadequate	Unworthy
Deceived	Insecure	Used
Defeated	Intimidated	Victimized
Deprived	Irritated	Vulnerable
Disappointed	Lonely	
Discouraged	Lost	
Disgusted	Manipulated	
Drained	Neglected	
Dread	Rejected	
Embarrassed	Resentful	

Over the years, many great authors, such as Louise Hay and Karol Truman, have written books about the correlation between specific emotions and the disease and dysfunction that is the result. These root emotions have been shown to cause the same symptoms over and over. It's really quite remarkable when you begin to understand that specific emotions and feelings can produce specific outcomes. Just as I discussed in the earlier chapter, your environment or the thoughts you think can affect how your nervous system responds. When you consider that, is it too big a stretch to believe that particular root emotions can cause a specific nervous system response and pain/disease pattern? Although it may sound pretty farfetched, I've found in my practice that these identified emotions are usually pretty accurate in describing what these people feel on an inner level and the conditions that have manifested.

Here are some examples of common pain patterns and the underlying emotions. Take a look, and see if any of the emotions relate to you.

(Taken from Louise Hay and Karol Truman's books)[1]

Pain	Emotional Root
Aches	Loneliness, feeling that nobody loves me, sadness
Ankles	Fear of falling or failing, inflexibility, instability
Arms	
Left	Not bringing spirituality to yourself
Right	Not doing enough physically for yourself
Arthritis	Holding onto hostility and anger, long-term tension and anger, depression, rigid thinking and feelings, uncompromising
Back Problems	Feeling unsupported and burdened and frustrated
Upper	Emotionally unsupported and burdened, agitated and anxious

[1] Karol Truman, *Feelings Buried Alive Never Die* (Las Vegas, NV: Olympus Distributing, 2003), 226–72; Louise L. Hay, *You Can Heal Your Life* (Carlsbad, CA: Hay House 1999), 176–221.

Middle	Guilty, lacking self-confidence
Lower	Unsupported financially, fear of lack of money, running away from a situation or wanting to back out of something
Bursitis	Anxiety, repressed anger, feeling loss of control, helpless
Chest	Unresolved fears, lack of self-love, feeling unprotected, hurt where love is concerned
Chronic Fatigue/ Fibromyalgia	Feeling alone, despair, hopeless, low self–worth
Disc	feeling indecisive about life, feeling no support in life
Feet	Fear of the future and stepping forward in life
Hands	Problem with grasping or letting go of ideas
Left	Receiving or being passive
Right	Fearing new ideas, fearing lack of opportunities
Headaches	Inability to resolve emotional issues, unexpressed hurt feelings, inability to face an issue or have control
Indigestion	Feeling everyone is against you, anxiety, fear of losing security
Inflammation	Rage, anger, or fear
Jaw/TMJ	Rage, subconsciously wanting revenge, inability to express feelings
Knee	Not wanting to bend, ego and pride get in the way, stubbornness
Left	Insecurity, unresolved stress
Right	Need to be more assertive, Not wanting to give in to authority
Leg	Fear of moving ahead in life, fear of change

Muscle Cramps	Stubbornness, resists moving forward
Muscle Pain	Guilt, not being good enough
Neck	Unable to let feelings out, nonacceptance and rejection of others
Sacroiliac	Feeling that you are in the wrong place
Sciatica	Overconcerned with money issues, being double-minded, sexual frustration
Shoulder	Bearing burdens that don't belong to you, carrying stressful responsibilities, lack of courage
Left	Relates to family stress
Right	Relates to financial stress
Spine	Feelings of shyness, inferiority, not standing up for yourself, afraid to live your feelings
Spurs	Built-up resentment
Stiffness	Inability to give, inflexible to opinions and attitudes of others, rigid feelings
Wrists	Imbalanced in giving and receiving, holding on to outmoded beliefs about life and self

When looking at your pain patterns in the chart and the root emotions, do you find that those feelings describe you in some way? If so, those are the key emotions you want to start with. If those emotions and feelings don't resonate with you, or you don't find any truth in them, don't worry. There could always be another related emotion that is charging your pain. The above list is just a starting point.

You may be thinking that the correlation is just found because the chart gives people something to believe, and because they are so desperate for help, they just make a connection. That may be true to some extent, but when we work through the POP Method steps, they still get results.

Do you have any feelings that resonate with you when you think of the pain? Maybe it's not just one but several emotions that come up. Those can all be explored further. Notice if any situations or scenarios from your past come to mind as well. Think about your pain, and then open your mind to your past. Does anything pop into your head? What was happening in your life when this pain started? Were there any situations that you remember vividly when the pain began? It may not be anything that directly caused the pain to start, but because you never dealt with the feelings surrounding that situation, the pain that was caused by something else became chronic because of these anchoring emotions.

When you think of your pain, how do you feel about it? Think about what feelings may be giving it that staying power. When you think of a situation from the past and it still gets you upset, that is a good place to start. Those emotions have power. Those unresolved feelings could be the key to why you can't get rid of your pain.

Many times when you are doing this exercise, an old memory will surface. Maybe at the time it didn't seem like a big deal. Well, take note—you are remembering it for a reason.

With this process of examining your feelings around the pain, the events or thoughts that come to mind are significant. Maybe an emotion you are feeling is irritation that you even have to deal with this pain; that irritation and frustration can be an anchor.

There is always an idea behind a manifestation, whether it be positive or negative. The key to overcoming your pain is to get back to that thought, that idea, that feeling, and then change the way you feel about it. (But, that's step 3, so we will get to that later.)

The saying, "What we think about, we bring about," comes to mind, and that is our reality. By becoming aware of the emotions and thoughts that are on autopilot in our minds, our whole bodies will change; our pain will disappear, our bodies will change, and our lives will become completely different. When our feelings change, our world changes too.

Now that you have begun to identify those emotions and stories that relate to the pain, those emotions that became anchors, you are ready for the next step.

The thoughts we choose to think are the tools
we use to paint the canvas of our lives.

—Louise Hay

CHAPTER 4

Step 2: Asking the Tough Questions

Tough Question 1: Why is this emotion still charged up?

O nce we identify the problem and some of the emotional roots associated with it, we must then examine what is giving it such power over our bodies. The first question we must ask when it comes to an emotional anchor is, "Why is this feeling still charged up?" What is giving it that staying power? It could be that you have never dealt with those feelings, just pushed them down deep. Remember stuffing? Just because they aren't right there at the surface reminding you they are there doesn't mean that they have been dealt with or resolved. Often we stuff some of our most difficult emotions down because, at the time, we just don't want to feel them so acutely. That makes sense from a survival aspect, but those emotions that aren't resolved can fester—and in this case, that festering has developed into chronic pain.

For many of us, we didn't do anything to start the pain, but it just appeared one day and didn't leave. That emotional root began to manifest into something tangible. It may have developed years after the feeling was experienced. One reason for that is because our bodies are fantastic compensators. Our bodies can handle dysfunction for a long time before the pain ever sets in. That's why, from a chiropractic standpoint, we like to evaluate people even when they don't have pain because pain is a terrible indicator of dysfunction. Many times pain is the very last thing to show up. With that in mind, some of the key emotional anchors may be feelings from a long time ago that were never recognized and dealt with. That is why in the previous chapter I said that although the emotions might not have a rational connection, it is still worth looking at.

Sometimes, understanding what is charging up the pain requires a little detective work.

Start to evaluate those key feelings and think about what event or situation spawned it. Was it something that changed the course of your life? Did it change the way you felt about yourself or others? If so, this may be the reason it is still charged up and staying anchored. These feelings may have become a part of your identity, so your subconscious mind doesn't want to let them go. We will talk more about how to resolve these types of feelings in a later chapter.

In order to really examine the staying power of these emotions, and more specifically, the emotions and feelings connected to the pain, we have to first quiet our outer selves, our *physical* selves, and focus on our *spirit* selves. This is sometimes the hardest part of the method. Have you ever tried *not* to think? It's tough! But connecting to our spirit selves, that perfect energy within us, and allowing that part of us to reveal things we have buried, is the key. Your spirit wants to help you and speak to you, but the only way for that to happen is to quiet down everything else. By taking some time for contemplation and meditation, you are giving permission to your soul to speak.

There are many different methods of meditation, and any type will work, as long as you are finding that quiet space within. If you have never tried to meditate, begin with taking just a short period each day to focus on mind clearing, and then lengthen that time period in small increments each day.

If you are new to meditation, here is a method that works for me. I begin by finding a nice, quiet, peaceful spot. Taking a few deep, cleansing breaths— in through my nose, out through my mouth—I allow my chest to expand completely. Once I start to feel calm and peaceful, I envision a beautiful blue sky and a crystal-blue ocean with waves gently rolling in. As I take those deep, cleansing breaths, I imagine that all of my thoughts are rising up on the crest of a wave and then being drawn out to sea—breaking all of my ties with those thoughts and images. In through my nose, out through my mouth, all the feelings and thoughts that have been creating endless chatter in my head are being drawn out to the ocean, never to be seen again.

If this process doesn't completely quiet my mindless chatter, I then envision a huge, open sky with a powerful wind coming up on my left side and pushing all of my thoughts out of my right side, into the breeze, releasing it into the wind. The key to any method you use is finding that calm space to allow your soul to open up. Stillness is the key.

Once you have settled the chatter and found a peaceful space within, it's time to get centered and focused on what feelings and emotions are causing you so much pain. To help you bring focus to your body, you can take both hands and place the tips of your fingers along your forehead, right over each eye. While continuing to stay in that quiet space, you can begin to ask yourself some questions:

Questions to consider:

- Why am I allowing these feelings to have power?
- Why are these emotions staying anchored?
- Why am I holding on to this pain?
- What about these feelings and this pain gives them strength?
- Why am I keeping these feelings inside instead of letting them go?

Focus on these questions, and pay close attention to what comes to mind. Maybe you see a scene being played out in your head. Or maybe you have a feeling come over you. Whatever feelings, images, or thoughts come to mind, remember to write them down for further examination. Think about those emotions from the chart that you reviewed in the previous chapter, especially the ones that seemed to evoke a response or memory in you. Why are those feelings charged, and why are you giving them staying power? While your mind is clear of the chatter, you can allow your spirit self to speak to you. Let it guide you and show you what key emotions are causing you pain and dysfunction. Take whatever images or feelings you have during this time, and feel the truth in them. When you can, write them down.

When first starting this exercise, nothing may come to mind. That's okay. Just take some time and be still. Maybe for now mindfulness is what you need most. Take some time to enjoy your stillness and any random thoughts that come to mind, acknowledge them, and then let them go. If you get no vivid memories or strong feelings at this time, be grateful for the stillness, step away from it for a while, and then return and try again.

Maybe you did get an image in your head, but it didn't hold much relevance to your situation. Or maybe you can't see any way that those feelings are associated with your pain. That's okay—it will all become clear soon enough. Write down whatever comes to mind and record the charge or the intensity of the feelings around the image or thought. If it evokes a response in your body when you think about it, whether it be increased heart rate, muscle tension, or any other shift in your body, note it. It may not evoke a physical response but instead be a thought or feeling you just can't let go of. That gives you an indicator that this is a charged feeling. It has some power over you and has become anchored for some reason. Take the time to really feel those thoughts and circumstances and write down everything that comes to mind.

Sometimes you have to dig deeper.

If you are still having trouble understanding these feelings and why they are rooted in you, you can use a stream of consciousness method to allow your thoughts to come to the surface. This method starts with finding that same quiet space but then using a pad and pen to write down everything that comes to mind. You can even write in big, bold letters at the top of the page: "Why are these feelings holding on?" Write down anything and everything that comes to mind, no matter how insignificant you think it may be. Write it down, and keep working through the steps of the method.

This stream of consciousness method is what allowed me to write this book. The words just started pouring out of me once I found that inner stillness and let my soul speak. This is a great daily practice to incorporate into your life. Powerful insights can come to light. For your chronic pain, though, use that quiet space to allow those innermost feelings to be revealed and for those emotions to surface.

Still having trouble?

If nothing seems to be coming to you, go back to the lists from the previous chapter and see what words pop out to you at the time. Use the questions above, and see what is revealed.

No matter what method you use, if you get quiet, allow that internal chatter to settle, and really listen to what the innermost part of you has to say, you will find that inherent cause. Just trust in the process and continue to follow it, and soon the message will be clear. If you don't get anything at all, you can move on to the next question, and once you finish the rest of the steps, focusing solely on the pain itself, go back and start the process over. Many times that will open up your consciousness enough to allow those underlying emotions and feelings to become transparent. Sometimes, even while you are in the middle of finishing the rest of the steps, the revelation will appear. Just follow through with the process.

Okay, now it's time for Tough Question 2: "How Does This Pain Serve Me?"

At first glance, your reaction to this question would probably be that this pain doesn't serve you at all. Why would we want to have pain? It's hard to imagine that our bodies would intentionally hold on to something that hurt.

But let's take a moment to think a little more about this question.

*How does this **serve** me?*

Let's consider for a moment that pain could be an excuse. When you think about what your pain can get you out of, isn't that serving you in some way?

I was just speaking to a patient the other day about this. She was telling me how much she wanted to lose weight. I asked her what she was doing to make that happen. She said that she couldn't really do anything because she hurt so much! Of course, that wasn't completely true—she *could* start with writing a diet diary and controlling portions, eating more nutritious, healthy foods, and so on, but being able to lose weight in her mind was only possible if she exercised, and she couldn't do that because of her pain. The pain gave her, on some level, an excuse for being overweight. It was *serving* her.

Another example of pain serving you could be a more physical excuse. For instance, maybe you are a homemaker and everyone expects you to take care of everything around the house. Maybe you are tired of people expecting that from you. With the pain you are having, the other family members have to pick up the slack and you are happy to have the load a little lighter! The pain is serving you.

I had a patient who had chronic, debilitating pain for many years, and no matter what she did, she couldn't get any relief. She had been to countless doctors, and they had diagnosed her with a rare nerve condition, but their conventional treatment had no result. They couldn't explain why the pain was so intense. It was holding on, and nothing helped. When she finally came to see me, we made some progress with her pain through chiropractic treatment, but the pain would return. She was so depressed and down, and she really was at the end of her rope. I had just started to develop this method, and it wasn't complete, but I felt the need to delve into the emotional side of her pain because I really believed that the *feelings* around her pain were what kept it holding on.

Now, please understand that this person had tried medical treatment for years. She had exhausted all possibilities from a medical standpoint for her care. And although I advocate using the POP Method for many health problems, I am in no way suggesting that other treatments should not be followed. This particular patient had exhausted all those options all ready.

To begin to uncover her anchored emotions, I started to ask her some of the tough questions. When I asked her what emotion she identified with the pain, she really could not think of anything at first. We began to talk about what was happening when she first developed her symptoms, and she described a time of great loss. Several family members had passed away, one after the other, and the grief was a tremendous burden. She also had a lot of anger and bitterness around these circumstances, and the more she talked about it, the more upset she got.

After identifying the situation at the time the pain started, and the feelings associated with it, we then began to talk about the pain. We then moved on to how this pain could be serving her. Of course, the first answer she gave was, "It doesn't." But then she took a minute to really think about it. First and foremost, her chronic, debilitating pain gave her something else to think about and worry about. With all the loss in her life, and the unbearable grief associated with it, she needed an outlet, and the pain gave her that. The pain was serving her. Not only that but the grief and loss had become her new identity. It was deeply anchored as a part of her being. Without it, who would she be? And further holding on to that grief and that identity in turn made the pain hold on as well.

Not only did the pain give her something else to think about but it also provided a way for other people to pay attention to her and make her "special."

Because she had a rare condition, on a subconscious level, it gave her a way to feel important. It was serving her by keeping attention on her because without it, on some level, she thought she would be lost or forgotten, just like her loved ones. And if she let go of the pain, she would also be letting go of them in some way. It was serving her.

Do you see how pain and emotions can serve us? Reflect on how your pain may be serving you. Be still and think about the excuses your pain allows you to justify. I bet when you really allow yourself to think on this level, you can come up with a few ways your pain serves you and your choices.

Here are some questions to ask yourself:

- Does my pain allow me to get out of things I really don't like to do?
- Does my pain give me the right to be lazy?
- Does my pain get me more attention?
- Does my pain help me feel special?
- Has the pain become how I identify myself?
- Does my pain give me an excuse for the way my life is?

When we answer these questions honestly, most of us will find some truth in them. Of course, from a realistic point of view, no one really wants to hurt … but can't you see how on a deeper, subconscious level, we may want the pain to hang on for a while?

Once you begin to unearth some of these deep-seated feelings, I encourage you to seek some professional therapy as well. The POP Method is a great start and can be very effective, but it does not replace professional counseling. Depending on how buried and significant these issues are, discussing this with a therapist can make this process even more profound. This book is a way to increase awareness of the possibility of some hidden anchors and to allow you some self-exploration, but sometimes deeper work is needed.

As we continue on with our exploration of our anchored feelings and how they can serve us, consider this idea. Have you ever noticed that when you go to the doctor and you get a diagnosis of something really rare or unusual, you want to go tell others about it? On some level, you feel special because of the problem you have. It may seem odd to believe that we are holding on to our pain, but many times, that is exactly what we are doing. It feeds our egos and charges that human part of us that wants to be unique.

Ask the tough questions, and examine how your pain is emotionally charged. Examine thoroughly how it could be serving you. It doesn't have to be rational, but it could be your truth on a subconscious level. Don't worry. You don't have to show it to anyone. But do write down what you discover. Just the process of getting it on paper can make a tremendous shift. Sometimes writing down and facing the feelings and events that are the root of your pain can be difficult. And of course, we avoid things that appear difficult, but this is necessary, and it won't be as hard as you think. It actually can be freeing. When you finally acknowledge something that has been with you for so long and has caused problems for you, you take its power away. You are taking charge of your life and taking away the charged emotions in the process. You are beginning to loosen the root and its anchor. You are beginning to put the power back in your hands.

Now, if through this process you haven't discovered a way the *pain* itself has served you, maybe it is the *situation* instead. Maybe it's the feelings, emotions, and circumstances that triggered the pain to start in the first place that do. Go back to your list of feelings that you associated with the pain. Look at those emotions, and ask yourself: "How do these feelings serve me? How does holding on to the feelings surrounding this situation identify or serve me?" Go through all of the questions listed above, and ask them concerning the event or circumstances you have identified to be a part of your pain.

Do this even if you have already found reasons that the *pain* has been serving you, because the *feelings* around the event that started it may be fueling the fire.

One example of a feeling you may believe serves you is anger. Maybe holding on to your anger about a situation fuels you to work harder. Maybe you believe that the anger is what drives you, and if you lose that, you will also lose your motivation to get ahead. Or maybe the feeling is loneliness. By hanging onto that feeling, you remember to never let anyone get close to you so you won't feel abandoned if they leave.

On some level, in some aspect of your consciousness, you believe these problems serve you or you wouldn't still have them. You identify with these feelings and this pain, and your subconscious mind and your ego do not want to let it go. Ask these tough questions and really answer them honestly, because this one step can open up a new world of possibilities.

If you change the way you look at things,
the things you look at change.

—Wayne Dyer

CHAPTER 5

Step 3: Reframing the Pain

I t's now time to put a new spin on those feelings you've identified as emotional anchors. With the hard part out of the way, now you can focus on making the changes and shifts necessary to loosen the hold those feelings have on you and lessen the pain as well. You've made it through the difficult part of the method, so now it's time to reap the rewards.

This third step in the POP Method is called reframing. When we reframe something, we take something that looks one way and change it to make it look better. We see it in a different light, so to speak. Let's start first with the feelings behind the pain. Even though on some level we can justify having these feelings, let's take those thoughts and change them a bit.

For instance, let's go back to the feeling of being angry. Although in some ways those feelings give you power, and they may be justified in some way, let's imagine what would happen if you let the anger go. Just for a moment, imagine how you would feel if you no longer had the anger. How would you feel inside? Is the feeling freeing at all? Is any of your power actually gone? What if by letting that go, it gave you more power over yourself and others? What if it made you stronger? Imagine your world and your interactions on a daily basis with those you have had this intense anger toward. How would you *be* around them without all the hurt and animosity? How would you be with others? More open maybe? Or more understanding? Ask yourself what it would be like if you lived your life as if that situation had never happened at all.

In Wayne Dyer's Book *Excuses BeGone!,* he speaks in depth about all the excuses we have developed in our lives and how those beliefs have shaped what we have become. He goes on to show us how to dispel every one of them and then how to imagine our lives to be without them.

> I invite you to try on a new lens that lets you access your false self with its ton of excuses and its belief in limitations. As it edges God out, your false self forces you to part with ideas that prove you're a spiritual being having a temporary human experience. Ego gives you a rationale for creating the rationalizations and justifications that eventually go on to direct your life. They become so embedded in what social scientists call the subconscious that your habitual mind turns into an excuse machine.[2]

Dyer goes through a process of looking at your beliefs and answering a series of questions and steps that essentially help you with *reframing* those same ideas so you can achieve the life you have only dreamed about. One of his key questions is, "Is it true?" And going even further, "What would your life be like if

---

[2]   Wayne Dyer, *Excuses Begone!* (Carlsbad, CA: Hay House, 2009), 24.

it wasn't?" Those are pretty powerful questions, and they can change everything in your life!

Imagining What It Would Feel Like to Let Go

One way to loosen this emotional anchor is to imagine what your life would be without the root feeling. Let yourself picture what letting go of all those key feelings and emotions, those beliefs and excuses, could do to your relationships, your inner peace, your life. Imagine how things would be and feel if you let those charged-up emotions go. Really try to get a clear image of what that looks and feels like. Let your imagination be in control for a moment.

Here are some questions to ask yourself:

- If I didn't have these anchored feelings, how would my life be different?
- If I viewed this situation from someone else's point of view, would he or she view the situation in the same way I do?
- If these feelings didn't exist, how would I feel about that?

- If these feelings were no longer true to me, what could my life be like?
- If I treated the people around me differently, how would my life change?

When you are looking at the events that may have started the pain, you may find that you blame someone else for what happened. Maybe just thinking about that other person gets you all wound up. Try looking at the situation from that person's point of view, and try to come up with reasons why he or she may have acted the way he or she did in that circumstance. Try to see the other person's side. Ask yourself, "What if he or she acted that way because _____?" Try to find a reason why that person may have done what he or she did. Give that person the benefit of the doubt that he or she didn't hurt you intentionally, and then look at the situation again. Do the emotions surrounding the event feel the same?

Imagining Yourself Pain-Free

Next, take the feeling of pain that you have and imagine what being rid of it would do for you. See yourself pain-free. What does that look and feel like?

As I mentioned in the last chapter, our thoughts shape our lives, so just this imagining process can begin the shift away from your painful life to a pain-free one. It can begin to loosen that anchored emotion and pain. Take a few moments to feel a new you.

What if the pain no longer *served* me and being pain-free *saved* me?

Did you know that in seven to ten years, almost every cell in your body is a new one? Some cells are new many times over in a year. Also, do you recall when I said earlier that thoughts can change the way cells react? Those thoughts are creators, remember?

With that in mind, realize that every second we begin to think and act differently, we can create brand new cells that function differently and in turn, make us feel different. Our bodies are changing every second of every day, so let's use that to our advantage and start changing the way our bodies' new cells look. Let's become healthy; the new cells that form don't have to be the same as before. We just have to start creating a better picture of what we want to become. And we do that starting with our thoughts and our feelings.

Imagining the Self You Want to Be

This is where the reframing comes in. Take some time to ponder, "What if?" Just for a few moments: "What if I no longer held onto these feelings? What if I let go of this pain? What if I woke up feeling like a teenager tomorrow? What if I won the lottery?" (We can dream, right?)

Buddha says it perfectly: "What we are today comes from our thoughts of yesterday, and our present thoughts build our life of tomorrow: our life is the creation of our mind."

Just as this quote suggests, thoughts are powerful and creative. Everything in our world started with a thought. Daydreaming and imagining things can be the start of something new and wonderful in your life. Don't think of this reframing process in the context of being a waste of time. It is crucial to get your brain in the game. By seeing in your mind's eye what *could* happen if you no longer had the pain or the feelings associated with it, the most powerful, creative machine on this planet is helping you achieve your goal.

One exercise I like to use with my patients is solely for the purpose of getting their brains in the game. I ask my patients to bend down and touch their toes. I record how far they can bend. Then I ask them to imagine themselves as if they have rubbery, stretchy muscles that are superhuman—to imagine themselves in their mind's eye being able to bend forward with straight legs and place their palms flat on the floor. Once they get that picture in their mind, I have them do the forward bend stretch again. Guess what happens? Each and every time my patients do this mental exercise, their forward-bending flexibility improves! They are letting their brains get in the game—and the brain wants to produce on the outside whatever picture or image it gets on the inside. This can be done with any movement in your body. Have fun with it and see what your body can do. Your brain wants you to accomplish everything you imagine, and it knows no bounds. Let it help you reach your goals and get beyond the pain.

Your brain is amazing. And one thing we can use to our advantage is the fact that it doesn't know reality from make-believe. It just takes thoughts and creates from that. Isn't that fantastic? Whatever you think you can create! Do you see how powerful and life-changing that one piece of information can be? By just changing what you are thinking, you can ultimately change your entire being.

But wait—always remember the flip side. As we have seen in earlier chapters, thinking about the pain and fear and hurt and anger ... it gets you more of the same, right? You get more pain and fear and hurt and anger! So let's use our reframing to change those emotions and loosen that anchor a little more.

What if every night you were able to supercharge your positive thoughts and images, allowing you subconscious mind to begin their creation? One way to do that is to start every night before bed imagining your life as if it were perfect. Those last thoughts before bed stay at the forefront of your mind for hours while you are sleeping, creating while you are catching your ZZZZs. Let your brain help you get everything you want. Keep giving it those perfect images to create, and recognize that the more you form those beautiful images and imagine them as if they have already happened, you are that much closer to getting there. Forget getting caught up in what is wrong with your world, and instead imagine what your world will look like when everything is right. Reframe your feelings, and create the future of your dreams.

Trade your expectations for appreciation and your whole world changes in an instant.

—Tony Robbins

CHAPTER 6

Step 4: Practicing Gratitude

O nce we have begun to imagine and create a more favorable picture of our lives and those rooted emotions have begun to lose some of their ground, we want to then uproot all of those remaining pieces and flood our bodies and minds with positive feelings so that the feelings and pain are more easily released. Practicing gratitude is great way to accomplish that.

Having gratitude is something most of us have been brought up believing in. Most of us were taught to always say thank you when we were given something, to be thankful for what we have, and so on. We even have a holiday called Thanksgiving.

But how many of us make that a priority? How many of us take time out of each day and practice gratitude? Some of us may count our blessings daily, but how many of us go further to give thanks for the things we don't exactly see as good at all? How many of us practice finding gratitude in everything we are given—the good and the bad?

There is a difference between being gracious and practicing gratitude. Most of us are very gracious when it comes to our interactions with people. But on an inner level, how often do we *practice* gratitude for who we have become, for our bodies, and even for our daily trials and tribulations and find ways to see each instance in our life as a *gift* we have been given?

Neale Donald Walsh, author of the many *Conversation with God* books, talks about this idea in length. He explains that when struggles happen, it is the perfect opportunity to express thankfulness and overcome those issues that hold you back. Be grateful you are being given the opportunity to gain mastery over your obstacles. For more spiritual growth and enlightenment, you have to be given more situations to master. These problems are your opportunities. The things going wrong in your life may be the exact thing you need to overcome in order to become a better version of yourself. Think of your pain and problems in a different light, as a chance to grow, and with this positive spin on it, watch the problems go away. *When you change the way you look at your life, your life will change as well.*

In college, I had an injury that reinforced this different perspective on life's challenges. While I was sitting on the sidelines of an intramural softball game, an overthrown ball hit me square in the eye. After the impact, my eye filled with blood, and with the increased pressure that it caused, as well as the impact of the ball, I had optic nerve damage that resulted in blindness of my left eye. Not only was my eye function impaired but the eye looked different on the outside as well; it didn't move the same as the other, it was slow to respond, and it stayed dilated all the time. It was a challenge physically because I developed severe depth perception problems, but even more difficult was the thought that people could look at me and tell something was wrong with my eye. Being only nineteen years old at the time, it was a real knock to my self-confidence, to put it mildly.

Surprisingly, as a result of this injury, I ended up finding my life's work. One of my life's greatest challenges presented me with a wonderful gift. That summer, I got a job as a nanny for a chiropractor, and because of the obvious impairment she noticed with my eye, she asked if she could evaluate me. With one adjustment, my eye constricted back down to normal, the normal movement returned, and I got all of my peripheral vision back in that eye. It was a life-changing moment for me. When I realized how powerful one chiropractic adjustment could be, I knew that I had to be a chiropractor and that I had found my calling. At that moment, I knew I needed to pay the healing forward. That injury, which most would have considered tragic, led me to a wonderful profession. And through that challenge, I learned to be grateful for all circumstances and struggles in my life. I was shown that everything that happens in our lives gives us the opportunity to learn and to become better versions of ourselves, not only by what we learn from the situation but how we view the challenge as well.

To find gratitude in your life and to really loosen the hold your negative emotions have over you, start to try and see your greatest struggles in a positive way. For instance, consider that if you didn't feel any pain, you wouldn't know what being pain-free really felt like. Without darkness, you would never truly understand light, so begin to view your problems as an opportunity rather than a punishment. Ask yourself, "How could this pain provide an opportunity for me? In what way has this chronic, ongoing pain taught me something, and what more do I need to learn from it?"

Maybe the pain gives you the opportunity to be more compassionate for others who suffer. Or maybe it helps you practice patience. Search for the gift in the challenge you are encountering.

Now, don't get me wrong. I do not believe that endless suffering is necessary for mastery, but if we begin to view difficulty as an opportunity for growth, it allows us to view life from a state of abundance rather than a state of lack. And when we view things from that perspective, we allow that perfect energy within ourselves to reveal and expand our opportunity for perfection. Consider this: if we didn't have struggles, how would we recognize our achievements and growth? As in my case, some of life's most challenging problems can become our greatest gifts.

One way to place your attention more on thankfulness and gratitude is to begin a gratitude journal. In a notebook, try to list at least three things each day that you are grateful for in your current life. Make a goal of coming up with new blessings every day forward. Also, use this journal to write blessings that may not have happened yet but that you would like to. The only trick to getting these to manifest is to write it as if it's already happening. Remember that your brain doesn't know reality from fantasy, so use it to your advantage. Be deeply grateful for all those things you wish for, and you never know, those exact things may become your new reality. Let your brain work for you and be a creating machine; that's what it's designed for.

Another way I practice gratitude is that I wake up each and every morning and give thanks for all of my many blessings and pray for many, many more. I also begin my day with a series of affirmations, setting my day up as if it is exactly how I want it. This is my beginning mantra each and every day. I have found that when I begin my day this way, even things that don't go quite my way tend to have little negative impact on me.

Some examples of my daily affirmations are as follows:

- I *Am* living my divine plan each and every day.
- I *Am* in perfect health and perfect form.
- I *Am* a healer, teacher, and guide.
- I *Am* a living example of love and light.
- I *Am* surrounded by people who love me and bring out the best in me.
- I *Am* financially free and give freely to those in need.
- I *Am* a vessel for healing with God's light and love, and I heal and Illumine everyone I touch.
- I *Am* God in action.

Create affirmations that include your gratitude and blessings, but also create new ones of how you want things to be. Just make sure they are written and repeated as if they are already a reality.

To further practice gratitude, I have created a vision board. I have a small poster board with many of my affirmations written on it, and beside each statement is a picture that represents it. Included on it are blessings I am currently experiencing, as well as some I wish for, but written as if they I am already living them. I have it in my closet so it is the first thing I see when I go to get dressed in the morning. I look at this picture board each and every day, imagining and feeling what these blessings realized look and feel like.

I first heard about vision boards from reading a book by best-selling author John Assaraf. He has a fantastic account about how powerful vision boards can be. In his book *Having it All,* he tells the story of when he was unpacking from his move into his dream house that his son uncovered an old vision board that he had made many years before. This board had been stored away, mainly because he had more recent ones that he was using, but on that particular stored-away vision board was an actual picture of the house he was moving into. It had been published in a magazine years before, and he had cut it out and posted it on his board. He hadn't seen that vision board in years and said that he really didn't even remember that picture, but on some level, his brain had remembered it. Through that vision board process, he had created his dream.

When practicing gratitude, whether it be through a gratitude journal, daily affirmations, or vision boards, we are giving ourselves a chance to create and develop our life experience. We are approaching the world from a standpoint of expansion rather than restriction.

With each step we take to feel more positive in our world and the situations and circumstances that are presented to us, the more uprooted the negative emotional anchors become. The more our beings are flooded with those positive feelings and images, the less room those emotional weeds have to root. And as those rooted feelings lose their grip, so does the chronic pain.

When I let go of what I AM,
I become what I might be.

—Lao Tzu

CHAPTER 7

Step 5: Releasing the Pain for Good

*L*et it go, let it go, don't hold it back anymore … The *Frozen* theme song plays in my head every time I think of this step. When you really think about it, all the stress and pain in your body are things you have refused to let go of. If you let go of those feelings and allowed yourself to live without them, wouldn't you feel better? Remember those images that you discovered when you thought about your life without those anchored emotions? That life imagined without the pain? Well, now that you have loosened their hold on you, you can take that final step to release them from your body.

Just like the rooted emotions and feelings, if you allow your inner self to let the pain go and no longer allow it to have power over you, you will be creating a new self; you are giving your body permission to heal.

You probably remember the saying, "I carry the weight of the world on my shoulders." Well, many of us have that feeling, and we get a lot of neck and shoulder pain (and other pain as well) because of it. That pain, that added weight we carry, can be gone if we choose to let it go.

I like to think of my body as a garment I can change in an instant. I believe that the true me is my spirit self, that inner part of me that is perfect and lives on forever. When I think of it that way, the pain can be given up just as easily because it is not truly a part of the real me; it is just the clothing I have created to cover my soul.

For some of you, it may be very difficult to view your body this way. The tangible part of you can be very convincing, especially when it is plagued with chronic pain. For those of you who feel that way, you are probably thinking, *How is my letting go* metaphorically *going to make changes* physically? I assure you, it is possible if you allow yourself to believe in a new way of thinking.

As a society, we have been trained to compartmentalize our problems into physical or emotional or spiritual, but they all blur together and are part of each other; when one aspect changes, the others will too. And to make it even easier, we have done the prep work to loosen the emotional roots that have charged this chronic pain and kept it active.

At this point in the process, you have discovered why you have the pain and why it has become rooted and anchored, you've put a new spin on it by reframing the feelings around it, and you have even found ways to practice gratitude and see opportunity in it. You've done all the hard work, so now it's time to release its hold on you and let it all go.

The final step in the Power over Pain (POP) Method is called the release. In this step, you will take that emotional anchor that has charged the pain and focus on it while touching the painful area. This allows your body to hone in and connect these two factors together. That way you can remove it all at once. By repeating a specific release script, you will then remove and release the pain and the feelings associated with it. During this process, you will be tapping over the heart center of your body (directly over the top portion of your sternum), getting to the heart of the matter, while also connecting with your subconscious mind and opening up and allowing yourself to let it go and let God do the rest. It's simple yet powerful.

So here we go:

1. Focus on your emotional anchor (all the feelings you have been working on).
2. Put one hand over the problem area, or if you have several areas, visualize your entire body surrounded with white light.
3. With the fingertips of your free hand, tap over your upper sternum lightly while reciting the release.

Here is the point that you tap on:

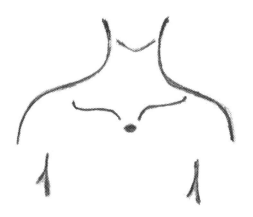

The release should be recited as follows:

Dear God, I love you and thank you
for all of my many blessings, and I pray
for many, many more. I call on you
now to take control, hold dominion,
and produce perfection in my body.
Release and remove, consume and
annihilate, all of the feelings of
_____ and
all of the pain it has caused me. These
feelings no longer serve me. They have
no place in my life anymore. Release it
all from me now, and replace it with your

pure and perfect love and light. Take it from me, and let me be free again. I *Am* healthy! I *Am* happy! I *Am* perfect just the way I *Am*! Thank you for taking it from me this instant and giving me the freedom to live my life to the fullest. I love you, and I thank you. Amen.

If speaking to God is not comfortable for you, here is another version of the release script that you can use:

As I stand here today, I *am* so very thankful for all of my many blessings, and I ask for many, many more. Today, I choose to connect with that perfect energy within me. I choose to let it take control, hold dominion, and produce perfection in my body. I choose to release and remove all the feelings of _____ in me and all of the pain that it has caused me. These feelings no longer serve me. They have no place in my life anymore. I choose to let all of these painful feelings in my body go and be replaced with perfect love and light. I allow my body to let go of it all this instant, and from this point forward, I am free from it forever. I *Am* healthy! I *Am* happy! I *Am* perfect just the way I *Am*.

As you finish the script, take a few deep, cleansing breaths, allowing your inner self to settle and your body to process the release. After a few moments, notice whether or not you are beginning to feel different—a change or shift in your body. Maybe you feel like a weight has been lifted off of you. Or maybe you feel like you can breathe better and have a better sense of peace within. Maybe the pain is less intense or gone. This is what I like to term a shift. Sometimes the shift you feel will be instantaneous. Other times the body has to process the release and it takes a little bit before you feel it. Have no doubt, though, that a change has occurred, and if it hasn't already, the shift is coming.

Many times, even while reciting the release script, overwhelming emotion comes to the surface. That is normal. Giving up something that has been tied to you for so long is significant. Acknowledge those emotions, and let them come out, along with all of the rest. This is a new beginning for you, a cleansing and rebirth, if you will, and allowing and accepting change is a challenge in itself.

Once you finish the release, check back in with yourself and the emotional anchor that you tied to the pain. Usually those feelings will no longer hold the emotional charge they once did. If there was an event or situation involved with the pain, notice your feelings around that circumstance as well. Most likely it won't feel the same. Sometimes a new emotion comes up, or you remember something you haven't thought of in ages that has some relation to the anchor you just released. If that happens, you go back to step 1 and start the POP Method over again with that new emotion.

Our bodies and pain patterns form in layers. Once one layer is lifted, sometimes another will surface. That is okay. A change is what we want to see. Even if the pain doesn't go away but moves, this is a shift. This is good. Even if a different pain surfaces, replacing the old one, that is all right. It means the body is responding and still processing. Change is good. You may need some deeper work, and to do that, you can always go back to the beginning step and work through the process again. Any change is a sign that the method is working.

Do not be discouraged if the change isn't instantaneous. I have had patients who felt no change directly after the release, but then the next day, the pain was gone. Of course, we all want things to feel better immediately, but we are complex beings and change can take time. The most important thing is to not give up because any shift, no matter how small, is a step in the right direction. You are one step closer to a pain-free life.

If absolutely nothing changes, give it time. Repeat the releasing step once a day for a few days, and then wait. If you still do not realize a change in the feelings or the pain, go back to step 1 and begin the method again. Maybe there is another emotional anchor that you haven't discovered yet. This will give your body more processing time as well, and a more significant shift should result.

Some of you may have felt uncomfortable reciting the release, and if so, you need to consider why that is. Maybe it does not feel true to you. You may not have loosened up that emotional anchor quite enough to allow yourself to let go of the pain. Go back to those earlier questions in step 2, and examine those feelings once again. You have to be ready to let it go, the emotional roots as well as the pain. If you are struggling with that, go back to chapter 5 and work on reframing some more.

This release step is very powerful. I have used this step of the method alone, without working through all of the other steps, and have seen remarkable results. When I do this, I first ask the patient to describe the pain and how having that pain makes him or her feel. We start with that emotion, focus on that, and then have the patient recite the release while touching the pain with one hand and tapping over the upper sternum with the other. Many times the pain clears and the feelings about the pain shift. It can really be that effective and quick. Of course, using the release by itself is effective mainly on more acute or recent pain because the emotions have not rooted as strongly, and the earlier steps give the release more power for those stronger emotional anchors.

But regardless, whether you work through the entire process or just use the release step for the acute cases, the POP Method works. I've seen it time and time again. Believe in the method and trust in the process, and it will work for you. You can heal your body. You can heal your life.

Each time you go through the steps, you are allowing yourself to chip away and rid yourself of the emotional baggage you have been carrying. Think of the release step as removing the old, outdated garment that has kept you from being your best. As you rid yourself of that, a new you is revealed.

Remember that you didn't get this way in a day, and you may not be healed in a day either. Whole-body healing is a process, just like the POP Method, and ongoing evaluation and work is necessary to become and stay in perfect health. Look at this as a lifestyle change that requires ongoing attention and support. You want to be the best version of yourself that you can possibly be. Each step you take toward feeling better, inside and out, is a step in achieving that. And with continued effort, the body and life you always dreamed of will be yours.

You can never cross the ocean unless you have the courage to lose sight of the shore.

—Christopher Columbus

Afterword

Allowing the healing of your entire body, the physical, emotional, and spiritual self, and bringing all of those parts back into balance is a powerful thing. You are not only overcoming a lifetime of chronic pain and limitation but you also are emerging as a better version of yourself and are able to live your life more fully. By having the courage to release all of the negative emotions and feelings that have anchored you to restriction and lack, you have allowed your inner light to finally shine through and be free.

We all face obstacles in life that may challenge us beyond what we think we are capable of, but in my experience, those very things are what help you grow emotionally and spiritually. Through my challenges, I have been given the opportunity to overcome and build a stronger trust in my inner divine self and my connection to all that is around me. I hope this method has helped you do the same.

No one should have to suffer in life, and hopefully this book has given you the tools to be free from chronic pain. Trust in the process to show you the way to live a pain-free life. When you believe, you can achieve. Don't let doubt be an obstacle to your healing. Use this time to develop your own connection to your higher self. Use this process to develop your feeling of connection to what is perfect within you, and expand that divine energy and reveal itself as your outer self. Shed the old garment, the body of restriction and lack, and become your true self.

I have learned through the development of this method that we are always connected to all that is and its powerful healing energy. It is always there, beating within our hearts and flowing through our bodies, but many times we aren't allowing ourselves to experience the perfection of that source. We can have it all if we just trust in being that perfection and let go of all the rest. That is what the release step is all about. We connect with our higher selves and that perfect part within us and let our pain and negative feelings be released and removed from us for good. Only then can we allow our inner perfection to be brought to the surface. It is always there; it is just obscured by all the discord and negative emotions we have piled on top of it. By removing the debris, that inner light shines brighter. The POP Method gives us a way to let God do his perfect work and to allow our perfection to be actualized. Now is the time for us to shine.

I am a true believer that we can change our lives in the blink of an eye if we want it badly enough. There is no magic pill to cure us, but instead the power is within. By following the five simple steps of the POP Method, you can change the way you feel in your body and in your world, and in turn, your body and world will change.

I hope this book has given you the tools you need to make lasting changes in your health and has freed you from the pain that has been holding you back. Anything is possible, and pain relief is only a few steps away. Take control of your life again and get power over your pain.

It is not in the stars to hold our
destiny, but in ourselves.

—Shakespeare

Frequently Asked Questions

How long does this take to work?

Many have used the POP Method once and the pain is gone for good. Others with more chronic cases have to work through several rounds of the process to relieve the pain and get it to last. Also, with any work of this nature, ongoing evaluation is beneficial. Revisiting the steps and working through the process can keep help maintain the results.

What is the difference between this and prayer?

I believe that step 5, the release script, can be viewed as a very focused form of prayer, while steps 1 through 4 allow you to discover and examine some of the core beliefs and feelings (emotional anchors) that are causing the chronic pain to remain. The POP Method gives you the tools to discover those roots and then gives you a way to call on divine assistance in removing them, so it could be a way to put more power into your prayers.

Can this replace professional therapy and counseling?

No, this is not a substitute for psychological therapy. The POP Method is a way to discover some of the emotions that are keeping your pain rooted to you, but it is not therapy. It is a tool to begin the journey of emotional exploration. And maybe it can give a different perspective to the emotional ties you may carry. Many times once you are able to recognize some of these feelings and triggers, counseling can help speed up the process of removing and releasing the emotional anchors. I urge those who are working through the steps to seek professional therapy if they believe they need some help working through the difficult emotions.

How can this method really work?

Honestly, I don't know! But it does. When I finally got out of my comfort zone and revealed this method to patients, the results were phenomenal. I still can't believe myself that it could be this easy.

What if I can't come up with any emotion or feeling behind the pain?

If you are having trouble with the emotions, that is okay. It is not every day that we are asked to analyze our feelings about something. Try to remember a situation or event that may have been occurring around the same time the pain started, and think about how that event may feel. That's a good start. If you still get nothing, begin to ask yourself the questions in chapter 4, and note anything that comes up. If you still do not come up with an emotion, use the release command and speak just about the pain itself. Usually, after the release you will feel a shift in the pain, and you often will then have a memory or emotion come to the surface. At that point, go back to step 1 and begin again.

Do you have to believe in God for this to work?

With this method, you do not have to believe in God for it to be effective. Just working through the steps and allowing yourself to let those anchors go can have a profound effect. I have even included an alternate release script for those of you who feel more comfortable leaving the spiritual emphasis out of it. The POP Method is most effective when you are able to feel comfortable with what you are saying in the release step, so use whichever version resonates with you. If you don't feel right saying the words, your body will have difficulty processing it. If you are agnostic, however, and do believe in a spirit/soul/and so on, you can just substitute whatever name resonates with you in place of "God," and read the first release script accordingly. This is a nondenominational process.

Do you have to go through every step of the process for it to work?

Sometimes you don't, especially if this is a pain that just started. If that is the case, you can find and identify the key emotion that is charging the pain and then move straight to the release step. Many times that is all you will need.

What if I don't notice any change at all in the pain?

Sometimes a shift in the pain takes time, especially if the emotional anchor is strong. Repeat the release script for several days, and if there still is no change in the pain, go back to step 1 and see if any more emotions surface. Those emotions may need to be released before your body can process them fully. Also, revisit the events and feelings that you found to be your negative anchors and roots. Have those feelings lost some of their power? Do you feel differently about them now? If so, that means you are making progress, and the pain relief will come. It is just taking your body longer to work through things. Continue working through the steps, especially the release step, until you get the shift in pain. Don't give up; trust that the process will work.

How is this different from EFT/tapping?

Tapping is amazing too. I have used EFT through the years, and it is phenomenal. The POP Method is different because of the process. Going through all five steps is different than the EFT process. The tapping over the upper chest plate/sternum is one of the tapping points in EFT, but the intention of it in the POP Method is more for opening the heart center rather than tapping acupuncture meridians. Also, this tapping point is a way to connect to the heart of the matter and keep the focus there.

Can the POP Method be used for something other than pain?

Definitely! My next project is to write about using this method for weight loss. Obesity commonly has an emotional root that manifests into a physical problem, and the steps of the POP Method can be used to change your views on weight as well. I am sure this could work with other disease processes as well, I just don't have any documented cases at this time. Just work through the steps of the POP Method and see what happens.

Printed in the United States
By Bookmasters